Hand Me That Hand Pie

Fifty Fabulous Recipes You'll Devour Hand Over Fist

Other Books by Deb Graham

Murder on Deck   a cruise novel

Peril In Paradise   a cruise novel

Tips From The Cruise Addict's Wife

More Tips From The Cruise Addict's Wife

Mediterranean Cruise With The Cruise Addict's Wife

Alaskan Cruise by the Cruise Addict's Wife

How To Write Your Story

How To Complain...and get what you deserve

Hungry Kids Campfire Cookbook

Kid Food On A Stick

Quick and Clever Kids' Crafts

Awesome Science Experiments for Kids

Savory Mug Cooking

Uncommon Household Tips

Contents

4

6

Tips And Tricks For The Best Hand Pies

What is a hand pie? A hand pie is a hand-held, single serving, perfectly portion-controlled bite of deliciousness, wrapped in tender, or flakey or chewy crust, just waiting for you to sink your eager teeth into its comforting goodness. They're cute, portable, and you don't even have to share. Ever been tempted to eat a whole slab of pie? With hand pies, go ahead, eat the whole thing, and you can still feel somewhat virtuous, because they're not big enough to blow your diet.

Homemade hand pies are satisfying to make, easy enough for a child to help, and loaded with your own fresh, wholesome ingredients. No canned pie fillings here! Hand pies are universal, and known by several names. Tarts, hand pastry, empanadas, mini quiche; if they're personal-sized, they're all good.

Some hand pies are elegant enough for a party, while others are great for a lunch box or after-anything snack. Need to bring a dish to a potluck? Hand pies fly off the platter! Fruit-filled hand pies are fancy enough for a baby shower, and a homey apple pie, personal-sized, will raise a friend's spirits faster than any old store-bought cupcake. Worried about your child getting enough nutrition in their school lunchbox? Pack a hand pie loaded with meat and vegetables, and they'll be fueled all afternoon.

Use local, fresh ingredients as much as possible. Is your garden bursting with butternut squash, ripe tomatoes, or leeks? Want to sneak some nutrition into your veggie-adverse family? Craving a warm, crusty delicacy? There's a hand pie for that! I guarantee whomever you're sharing the hand pies with will be delighted. In fact, the sense of accomplishment you'll get from baking your own hand pies is a treat in itself.

Plus, while luscious filling drips off your chin, know that you're touching history. Australians have eaten hand pies as long as they've been Australian, Cornish miners packed a version in their lunch pails, followed by West Virginian coal miners, who ate the filling, then threw the coal-dust-blackened crusts away. Pioneers scooped leftover stews into hastily-assembled lard-based crusts before resuming their long trek across the American plains.

I know you're eager to get baking, but first, a few **tips:**

Leaky hand pies are still delicious, but not impressive-looking. In every recipe except the ones baked in muffin pans, crimping the seams with a fork is an important step to prevent filling from escaping during baking. Just press the tines of the fork all around the edges.

Still, hand pies have a mind of their own, and some may leak. Parchment paper is a good investment, and less costly than those fancy silicone sheets, which do the same thing. Pies can't stick to it, and it's good up to 450 °F. Lining baking sheets will save hours of scrubbing stuck-on fillings off the pans; you'll thank me.

If you use muffin tins, here's a trick to get the pies out intact: Place a strip of parchment paper across the bottom of each indentation, with ends extending past the rim. For a regular size muffin pan, strips should be about 6" X 1". Make strips larger or smaller for bigger or smaller pans, obviously. After baking, lift the hand pies out of the pan using the paper as a handle. Magic!

Any unbaked hand pie can be frozen, tightly wrapped, with the lone exception of cream pies. I suggest wrapping the pies individually, then tucking them in a zip-type bag, so as not to lose them in the freezer. It can happen. Bake as directed, adding a few extra minutes to baking time. Go ahead and freeze leftover hand pies as well...if you have any left over.

Chop vegetables and other ingredients into small dice so they cook quickly and evenly. Always par-cook vegetables and other filling ingredients. If you skip this step, the pastry will over-brown before the filling is fully cooked. You'll regret it, trust me.

There are a just a few more tricks to successful hand pies. Make sure the filling is moist but not runny, thick enough not to leak out. A couple of small slits cut with a paring knife allow hot filling to steam, avoiding eruptions in the oven. Be sure to crimp edges with a fork. Be firm enough to leave a good fork-tine imprint. This is no time to be wimpy.

Don't overfill hand pies, or they'll burst at the seams. You want a good mouthful of yumminess, but if it's too messy, you'll need a fork, and that defeats the purpose of fun little hand pies. They're meant to be portable.

A fragrant hand pie fresh from the oven is a tempting thing, but if you can let the pies cool a few minutes, it will hold together better and you can avoid a blistered tongue from boiling filling. Especially in a sweet pie; that sugar is *hot*!

Once you are comfortable with making hand pies, let your imagination soar. Add pecans or walnuts for crunch. Pile cut cherries and chocolate chips on a crust, spoon last night's cooked chicken and chilled gravy in a pie, or layer Thanksgiving leftovers in a crust (don't forget a touch of cranberry sauce with the turkey and dressing!). Seal the crust, pop it in the oven, and get your taste buds ready. You're limited only by what your mind conjures up!

Feel free to change tastes and textures as you desire. With few exceptions, fillings and crusts can mix and match with abandon. You might want to avoid a spicy crust with blueberries, but that's entirely up to you. More on crusts in a bit.

Always preheat the oven. Start with a hot oven, lowering the temperature later in the baking process if they look to be browning too fast. The filling will steam and boil inside the crust as it bakes. You want the pastry crust to set up before the filling has a chance to bubble and ooze all over the place. If you see the pastry is browning too fast (before the filling is done), tent with a sheet of foil to prevent further browning.

Bake in the middle of the oven, or in the lower third. Hand pies need a sturdy crust, and this gives the bottom a better chance of cooking through before the top is overdone.

Brushing top of crust with a beaten egg or a little milk makes the finished hand pie a shiny thing of beauty. For a thicker glaze, mix powered milk with a little water; thicker than milk, thinner than a paste. A little coarse sugar sprinkled on a sweet hand pie makes a pretty finish, as well adding a nice crunch. Want to get even fancier? Mix a bit of lemon or lime rind with the sugar!

Decorating hand pies makes them even more appealing. After forming the pies, cut a shape with leftover dough and "glue" it on top with a bit of water. Use a cookie cutter to make apples, stars, hearts, letters, even fish, or go freehand with a paring knife. The possibilities are endless! Avoid delicate shapes; the pies will spread a bit in the over, and features may blur. And only do this with pastry; bread dough will make blobs; still tasty, but not gorgeous.

Common hand pie shapes include half-moons (folded circles), squares and rectangles, along with deep-dish versions in various sized muffin pans. Don't limit yourself!

What are you waiting for?

13

Crust is critical. Keep in mind your filling as you plan your crusts. Hearty fillings are best with a sturdy crust; save the lighter flakey crusts for delicate fillings.

If you're using a cooked filling, let it cool somewhat before assembling the pies to avoid melting the dough or pastry. Pastry needs to be cold when it goes in the oven. A yeast-based /bread dough will rise unevenly, or not at all, if too-hot filling touches it before baking. You don't want to annoy the yeast-beasts.

Hand pies have three main types of crusts: pie dough, puff pastry, and yeast-based bread dough. In general, delicate fillings call for delicate crusts, while heartier fillings can handle a heavier dough. Pie dough is bland, won't clash with soft or sweet fillings, and showcases fruit, egg, and other mild fillings beautifully. Puff pastry is delicate, made of many layers, prone to crumbling, doesn't transport well, and it's just the thing for an elegant setting. For lunchboxes and heavy fillings like stew and meat pies, your best choice is a sturdy yeast dough. Let's look at each.

Pie crust is reliable, fairly sturdy, and adapts well to many flavors. For savory pies, stir in a little pepper or grated cheese with the flour in the crust recipe.

You can make a batch or two of pie crust, form it into rounds and freeze it wrapped in plastic wrap. Thaw it as needed, or take a few minutes to make a fresh batch. It's as easy as...well...pie. Store bought pie crust is readily available, but unless you are physically unable to roll out dough, I don't recommend it. It has an artificial, chemical taste, tends to be waxy in texture, and I avoid ingredients I can't pronounce. By the time you drive to the store, pay for it and drive home, your hand pies could already be in the oven, encased in flakey, homemade crusts. I'll share my foolproof, super flakey pastry soon.

Puff pastry sheets are wonderful things! I've taken several pastry classes; I know how to make puff pastry. And I won't do it. The technical term is lacquered dough, named for its layers. The basic technique is a simple dough, rolled flat, spread with butter, folded like a book, wrapped, chilled, turned, rolled flat, spread with butter, folded like a book, wrapped, chilled...at least a half dozen times.

Speaking of time, mine is worth something, and I find store bought puff pastry to be just fine. It's tender, uniformly flakey, easy to work with, and you don't have to injure your biceps with all that rolling. Thaw frozen puff pastry in the refrigerator, unfold carefully, press together any cracks that may have formed, and shape, keeping cold until it's on the way to the oven.

Yeast dough can be handled rather roughly; let it rest a bit after the final rolling out to relax the gluten before you wrap it around filling. Be more delicate with pie and pastry dough; this is not the place to take out your aggressions. Any white or wheat bread dough recipe works great! Frozen bread dough is also fine, as are pre-baked tart shells or puff pastry cups.

Besides pie crust, bread dough, and puff pastry, you can also experiment with pizza dough or store-bought crescent rolls dough. Sliced bread pressed into a buttered muffin tin makes a decent crust in a pinch. Try a sugar cookie for a fruit tart, or phyllo dough for a Greek spinach-and-feta hand pie.

A few more pie crust tips:

Pie crusts made with oil are very forgiving. Ones that call for butter or shortening must be kept cold. As a rule, combine ingredients, then chill while you assemble the filling. Try to patch cracks in your dough rather than re-rolling the crust, or press together frail-looking areas. Over-handling makes the pastry tough. Tender is the goal!

Use the least amount of water possible, just enough to make the pie crust hold together. The recipe usually gives a range for the amount of water – start with the smallest amount, adding a bit more if needed. Letting the dough sit for few minutes will let the dough absorb the flour, letting you see if more is required.

Not sure how to roll out a pie crust? You can do it! I find it easiest to roll dough between sheets of waxed paper or inside a large zip-type bag, cut down the sides. You can also lightly flour the countertop where you plan to roll the dough. Pat the dough into a round, pressing any ragged edges toward the center.

Start your rolling pin in the center of the pie crust dough. Imagine the face of a clock, analog, not digital. Set the rolling pin where the hands meet.

Roll away from you toward the 12 o'clock position, easing up on the pressure as you near the edge; it's easy to make the edges too thin. Return the rolling pin to the center and roll toward the 6 o'clock position. Repeat rolling toward 3 o'clock and then toward 9 o'clock. Once it's a uniform thickness, about 1/ 4 inch, you're done! Now, cut hand pie shapes using a paring knife or wide cookie. Easy as pie!

Sizes And Fillings

Size matters! Appetizer hand pies should be about three bites each. Same with for super-rich or very sweet recipes; some are too rich for more than a few bites. Main dish pies can be larger, maybe palm-sized. Be sure to keep dessert hand pies single serving size. Sharing is not easy. If perfect uniformity is your preference, use a muffin tin to bake the crusty treats; they can't spread out of bounds that way.

For hearty picnic-meal-size meat pies, consider a mega muffin tin. They're ideal for Scottish meat pies; recipe to follow.

Once you're comfortable with a hand pie recipe or two, go ahead and play with sizes. A deep-dish pie baked in a muffin tin can easy convert to a round hand pie or half-moon shape. Mini tart size pies can be adjusted to fit a larger pan; just make sure the filling fits, and the edges are sealed. Bake in the middle of your oven, and adjust baking times, depending on size. As a general rule, bake until the crust is golden, the filling cooked, and your kitchen smells like heaven's bake shop.

Some recipes call for uniform, flat, open-face hand pies, like little tarts. Squares and rectangles are ideal for jam-filled hand pies. Folded half-moons enclosing a warm savory filling are appealing, and easy to hold. *Galette* is a fancy-sounding French word for rustic little free-form rounds with edges of the crust folded up and partway over filling. Some say "rustic" is another term for "too lazy to shape precisely," but it sure sounds better, doesn't it? Feel free to branch out with circles, triangles, rectangles...up to you so long as filling is contained and you can pick it up!

Hand pies can be savory or sweet. Both have their place; you can't live on dessert alone, not should you try. On a busy morning, grabbing a hot breakfast hand pie will set your day on a better track. Picky eaters may be tempted to try a cute little personal pie they helped make, whereas they'd starve rather than sample the vegetables hidden inside the bog pie Mom made.

Crust Recipes

Let's begin the recipes with the best pie crust out there. It's so easy, a child can make it!

Amazing Pie Crust

Versatile crust for just about any filled hand pie! This super easy, fabulously flakey, foolproof, brag-worthy pie crust will win raves, sweet or savory, and it's quick to make. Memorize it; you never know when you might be stranded on a deserted island and need a good pie crust recipe.

2 2/3 cups flour

1 1/2 teaspoons salt

3 /4 cup oil

4 1 /2 tablespoons cold water

Stir together flour and salt. Measure oil and water in the same cup, and pour over flour, all at once. Stir just until dough comes together, leaving some white streaks. Roll out between 2 sheets of waxed paper; it can be a little sticky.

Enough for about 24 small hand pies, or one ordinary-sized pie. Want to jazz it up? Add chopped herbs or citrus rind to the dough.

Old Fashioned Shortening Pie Crust

An old-standby type pie crust, suitable for either sweet or savory hand pies. be sure to keep the dough as cold as possible until it's in the oven. For even flakier crust, roll into three disks, wrap in plastic, and freeze at least one hour, then thaw before shaping.

1 1/ 2 cups vegetable shortening
3 cups flour
1 teaspoon salt
1 whole egg, beaten
5 tablespoons cold water
1 tablespoon white vinegar

In a large bowl, gradually work the shortening into the flour until no large pieces remain. Sprinkle with salt, then stir in beaten egg. Add 5 tablespoons of cold water, and 1 tablespoon of white vinegar. Stir together gently until no dry flour remains. Chill, then roll.

Sweet Butter Crust

This tasty, delicate crust must be kept cold until baked. Be sure your hand pie filling is chilled, too!

2 1/2 cups flour
3 tablespoons granulated sugar
1 teaspoon salt
2 sticks chilled butter
3/4 cup ice water, plus 2 tablespoons

Combine the flour, sugar and salt. Using a box grater, grate the cold butter into the flour mixture. Transfer to the freezer to chill for 5-7 minutes. Working quickly, break the butter bits into the flour with your fingertips until they resemble the size of small peas. Add 1/2 cup of water and mix. The mixture will be crumbly at this point. Add more water, a tablespoon at a time, until the dough comes together. Lightly knead a few times until it comes together in the bowl. Chill one hour (or longer) before rolling.

24

Make Your Own Pie Crust Mix

Want to save even more time? When you have a few extra minutes, mix together everything for your pie dough ahead of time: Combine flour, oil or shortening, and salt until it resembles peas. Transfer to a plastic bag, label, and store in the freezer for up to two months. Next time you want to make pie dough, dump the mix into a bowl, and just add water, a tablespoon at a time.

Straight Up Bread Dough

You can knead the dough in the food processor or by hand. I like doing it by hand, especially when I am having a bad day. It is a great way to vent anger or frustration. You can punch the dough, slam it against the table, get it all out, without anyone getting hurt. It'll only benefit the dough.

2 cups warm water (bathwater temp is fine)

1/3 cup sugar

1 1/2 tablespoons active dry yeast

 1 1/2 teaspoons salt

1/4 cup vegetable oil

6 cups white flour, or half white/half wheat

Bloom the yeast with water and sugar in a large bowl in a warm place until yeast resembles a creamy foam. Mix salt and oil into the yeast. Stir in flour, one cup at a time. Knead dough on a lightly floured surface until smooth. Let rise in an oiled bowl, covered, until doubled in size. This usually takes about an hour. Punch dough down. Knead until large bubbles are gone. Let rest a few minutes, then cut and shape.

Savory Hand Pies

The nice thing about savory hand pies is their versatility. You can make appetizers with any recipe simply by shrinking the recipe to two- or three-bite sizes. For a meal, make them about as large as your palm. Add a salad, and you'll have a tasty, easy meal!

Pepper-Steak Hand Pies

1 lb ribeye steak, sliced very thin
1 teaspoon olive oil
1 /2 onion, sliced thin
1 medium potato, cubed
1 bell pepper, sliced into thin strips
1 teaspoon Worcestershire sauce
2 thyme sprig
2 tablespoons flour
salt and pepper
1 /4 cup water
2 sheets puff pastry, thawed
1 egg, lightly beaten

Sauté beef, onions, potato and peppers until vegetables are tender. Stir in Worchester sauce, thyme, salt and pepper, flour, and water, and bring to a boil. Cool to room temperature.

Preheat oven to 425 °F. Cut pastry into squares. Spoon filling in center, fold to seal, and crimp edges with a fork. Cut slit in top to vent steam. Bake until golden, about 15 minutes.

Easy Summer Tomato-Cheese Galette

This is more of technique than a recipe, and it couldn't be easier! If you'd rather, press dough into a muffin cup. Drying the tomato slice prevents the little pie from getting soggy. No one likes a soggy pie.

Unroll refrigerated crescent roll dough. Separate into squares, pressing perforations together. Sprinkle any fresh herb, chopped, on each square. Top with hearty pinch of shredded gruyere or sharp cheddar. Pat dry a thick slice of fresh ripe tomato, and center on crust. Turn up edges, crimping to enclose, leaving top open. Sprinkle with black pepper, Bake at 425 °F until crust is golden.

Broccoli, Ham & Cheese Hand Pies

Yummy in a lunch box, or anywhere else! Dip in bottled honey-mustard salad dressing for extra tang

store-bought crescent rolls

1/ 2- 3 /4 pound cooked ham, chopped

1 1 /2 cups shredded mozzarella cheese

1 cup broccoli florets, chopped

1 tablespoon olive oil

1 teaspoon garlic salt

Preheat oven to 350° F. Unroll dough, cut into squares. Place some of the ham, cheese, and broccoli in the center of each square. Fold to seal filling, crimp with a fork to prevent leaking. Brush the tops with olive oil and sprinkle with garlic salt.

Bake for 15 minutes or until golden brown.

Overstuffed Mushroom Hand Pies

These are good warm or at room temperature, ideal for a summer picnic. Try different varieties of mushrooms next time.

1 puff pastry, thawed

1/2 onion, chopped

4 tablespoon butter

1 lb button mushrooms, sliced

2 teaspoon thyme, chopped

1 /4 cup broth or apple juice.

salt and pepper

1/4 cup grated gruyere cheese

Preheat oven to 400 °F. Cook onion in butter until slightly caramelized. Add mushrooms, thyme and broth or juice, and simmer until liquid evaporates. Cool to room temperature, then stir in seasonings and cheese. Gently roll out the puff pastry and cut into four even squares; smaller for appetizers.

Place a spoon of the mushroom mixture on each square, and fold to seal. Crimp edges with a fork. Place on parchment-lined tray. Bake for 15-20 minutes

Pepperoni Pizza Hand Pies

Ideal for an after school snack or a quick meal, these are faster than take-out, and delicious! Add your favorite ingredients to the filling. This has a soft, chewy crust; for a crunchier version, use bread flour.

1 package active dry yeast

1 teaspoon sugar

1 cup warm water (110 degrees F)

2 1/2 cups flour

2 tablespoons olive oil

1 teaspoon salt

2 tablespoons cornmeal (optional; makes crust crunchy)

1 /2 cup bottled pizza or pasta sauce

8 oz.. mozzarella, grated

Toppings: sliced pepperoni, cooked sausage, chopped peppers, ham, onions, etc, etc!

Preheat oven to 400 °F. In a medium bowl, dissolve yeast and sugar in warm water. Let stand until foamy, about 10 minutes. Stir in flour, salt and oil until smooth. Let rest for 5 minutes.

On a lightly floured board, pat dough into rounds, about 5 inches across and a half-inch thick (thinner if you prefer). Grease a baking sheet and sprinkle with cornmeal. Leaving a border spread a spoonful of sauce almost to the edge of each crust. Layer mozzarella and toppings. Bake in preheated oven for 15 to 20 minutes, or until bottom of crust is golden brown.

Chicken-Chili Empanadas

Hot, melty, cheesy, and just right for a light summer dinner! Serve with melon if you're sitting down, or grab these on the run

homemade double crust pie dough

8 oz.. cream cheese, softened

1 can (4.5oz.) chopped green chilies (don't drain)

2 cups chopped cooked chicken (or rotisserie or leftover)

1 cup shredded Monterey, cheddar, jack, or Colby cheese

Salt and pepper to taste

1 egg, lightly beaten

Preheat oven to 375°F. Stir together cream cheese, chilies, and chicken. Taste for seasoning. Cut pie crust into 5 inch rounds. Spoon a heaping spoonful of filling in the middle of each, and fold into half-circle. Seal edges with a fork. Make small slit in top crust, and brush with lightly beaten egg. Bake until golden, 15-22 minutes.

Corned Beef and Swiss Mini Pot Pies

A fun and festive play on a Reuben sandwich, these may be your new favorite hand pie. Ideal use for leftover March 17th meat. If you take them to a potluck, you'd better make extra, or you won't get any.

8 oz. cooked corned beef, coarsely chopped

1 cup shredded Swiss cheese (4 oz..)

1/3 cup sauerkraut

1 /4 cup mayonnaise

1 /4 cup sour cream

1 tablespoon Dijon mustard

1 teaspoon caraway seed

any bread dough recipe

Preheat oven to 375°F. Grease eight or ten regular-size muffin cups. In large bowl, mix corned beef, cheese, sauerkraut, mayonnaise, sour cream, mustard, and caraway seed until well combined.

Pat dough into muffin cups, keeping fairly thin, leaving some dough overhanging. Spoon meat mixture into each cup, 3/ 4 full. Fold overhanging dough partly over top, pleating in place, leaving some filling exposed. Bake 20 to 22 minutes until biscuits are golden brown. Cool slightly before removing from pan.

Mexican Meat Pies

These are so tasty, you'll want to go kiss somebody!
Ideal for a lunchbox or after-something snack!
They freeze and reheat well, so make plenty.

Amazing Pie Crust or any other pie crust

1 pound lean ground beef

1 onion, diced

2 cloves of garlic, minced

salt and pepper

1 teaspoon ground cumin

1/4 teaspoon ground cinnamon

1/8 teaspoon ground cloves

1 / 4 cup bottled salsa

1 cup canned tomatoes

1/4 cup raisins

1 egg, beaten

Brown the beef with onion and garlic, breaking apart as it cooks. Drain. Stir in seasonings. Add the salsa, tomatoes, and raisins, and simmer until raisins are softened and liquid is absorbed. Cool to room temperature.

Preheat oven to 425 °F. Roll half of the dough between 2 sheets of waxed paper into rectangle. Cut into three inch rounds, and place on baking sheet. Plop a tablespoon of filling on each circle. Roll out rest of dough, and cut equal number of circles. Brush edges of filled circles with beaten egg. Set top circle on each, and crimp tightly with a fork to seal edges. Cut slit for steam to escape in each pie. Brush remaining egg on top. Bake 12-14 minutes, until golden brown. Serve warm or at room temperature.

Great Greek Feta/Spinach Hand Pies

This is the recipe you've been waiting for! Salty, crispy, smooth filling...makes my mouth water just thinking about it! Best served warm.

1 packet dry active yeast

1 cup warm water

2 - 2 1/2 cups all-purpose flour

1 teaspoon kosher salt

2 tablespoons olive oil + 2 teaspoons for filling

2 cups spinach, roughly chopped

1 small yellow onion, diced

5 ounces feta, crumbled

Stir together the warm water and yeast in a bowl. Let stand for 5-10 minutes, until foamy. In another bowl, whisk together the flour and salt. Add the yeast mixture to the dry ingredients, along with the olive oil, and stir until dough comes together. You may need to add a little more flour if it seems too sticky.

Knead the dough on a floured surface until elastic and smooth. let rise in covered, greased bowl until dough has doubled in size, about an hour.

Cook onion and spinach in 2 teaspoons oil until spinach wilts. Cool and stir in feta.

Preheat oven to 425 °F. Line a baking sheet with parchment paper. Roll dough on a lightly floured surface to 1/4 inch thickness. Cut into 5-inch circles. Use a lid for a template to make them uniform. Set half of the circles on a parchment-lined baking sheet. Neatly spoon the filling into the center of each hand pie, leaving a border. Lightly dampen the edges with water. Top with remaining circles and firmly crimp edges. Cut slit to vent. Brush with olive oil, and let rest, covered, for 45 minutes. Bake until golden brown, about 20 minutes.

Alaskan Salmon Hand Pies

Elegant enough for a party, yummy enough for a light lunch! Great use of leftover salmon. Oddly, that's an issue in Alaska!

1 cup fresh cooked salmon, or 2 cans salmon, drained
1/4 cup chopped celery
1/4 cup chopped bell peppers
1/2 cup grated cheddar cheese
1 teaspoon fresh dill
1 tablespoon oregano
1 teaspoon black pepper
3 tablespoons mayonnaise
puff pastry dough, thawed

Combine all ingredients (except pastry—you knew that, right?). Unfold pastry, pressing creases. Plop filling in four equal mounds, evenly spaced, along the long side of the pastry dough, leaving a one inch border. Fold empty side of pastry over mounds, and press air out. Cut between mounds, place on baking sheet, and crimp edges with a fork, then slit top slightly to vent steam. Bake in preheated oven until golden.

Breakfast Ham and Cheese Hand Pie

Pie for breakfast? This grab-and-go hand pie is a meal in itself, and nearly virtuous. Make them the night before; they're good reheated or cold. And they're elegant enough for a fancy brunch!

frozen puff pastry, thawed

6 thin ham slices, chopped

3/4 cup ricotta

1 /2 cup grated mozzarella, plus more for topping

2 tablespoons milk

1/4 teaspoon nutmeg

salt and pepper to taste

1 tablespoon olive oil

1 medium onion, minced

1 clove garlic, minced

4 cups baby spinach, roughly chopped

1 egg, beaten

Preheat oven to 400 °F. Combine the ham, ricotta, mozzarella, milk, nutmeg, salt and pepper in a medium bowl. Set aside. Heat olive oil in a skillet over medium heat. Cook onion and garlic until fragrant, about 1 minute. Stir in spinach, cooking just until wilted. Remove from heat and combine with the ricotta mixture. Cut the puff pastry sheet into 4 squares. Place on the baking sheet and spoon the filling into the center of each. Gently fold up the sides of each square, pinching the corners together in the center. Brush each puff pastry with beaten egg and top with a sprinkling of extra mozzarella. Bake for about 15-20 minutes until golden brown around the edges.

On The Run Sausage-Egg Breakfast Hand Pies

Make a batch of these beauties and freeze them, then reheat on those mornings when you need a good hearty breakfast but don't have time to cook. Spinach is optional, but why not sneak in more veggies wherever you can?

Filling

1/2 cup onion, diced

8 large eggs, beaten

1 tablespoon water

1/2 cup grated cheddar cheese, plus a bit to sprinkle on last

8 ounces breakfast sausage

pinch of salt & pepper

1 /2 diced bell pepper

2 cups chopped spinach, optional

two sheets frozen puff pastry, thawed

Preheat oven to 375 °F. Sauté onion and sausage, breaking with a spoon, until browned. Drain fat. Whisk the eggs and water. Add eggs to pan, along with peppers and spinach. Cook, stirring frequently, until eggs are thickened but still moist. Add the cheese. Remove from heat.

On a floured work surface, roll out the puff pastry sheet, patting together any seams. Cut into 8-12 four-inch squares (depending on the size of your puff pastry sheets). If you have 8 squares, you may have a bit of leftover filling, which is a sudden snack for the cook. Place squares on a parchment-lined baking sheet

Evenly distribute the filling in the center of each puff pastry square. Fold up the corners of each puff pastry square so they meet in the middle. Gently pinch together the four corners and slightly flatten the filled pastry so it makes a square, distributing the sausage filling to the corners. Sprinkle the remaining grated cheese on top. Bake for about 20 minutes until golden and bubbly.

Spicy Ham and Cheese Hand Pies

*Don't fear the red pepper flakes; they mellow
during baking, and are perfect with the cheese and
ham. Great in a lunchbox. Make smaller for
appetizers, and make a lot, because they'll go fast!*

3 1 /4 cups flour
 1 /4 cup sugar
1 tablespoon instant yeast
1 1 /2 teaspoons red pepper flakes
1 1 /4 teaspoons salt
1 /2 cup warm water
2 eggs
4 tablespoons butter, melted
6 ounces Monterey Jack cheese, 1 /2 inch cubes
8 ounces cooked ham, cubed
 1 egg, beaten

In a stand mixer or large bowl, combine flour,
sugar, yeast, red pepper flakes and salt. Add warm
water, eggs, and melted butter. Knead until
smooth. Cover and let rise until doubled, about an
hour.
 Divide dough into 8 balls. Roll each into a half-
inch thick oval on lightly floured board. Arrange
cheese and ham evenly on each. Fold in half and
crimp edge with a fork. Let rest while preheating
oven to 350 °F. Brush with beaten egg. Bake until
golden.

Spinach and Artichoke Dip Hand Pies

You know that ooey gooey dip you love so much? Here it is, right in your hand!

3 cups spinach

1 1/2 cups finely chopped bottled or frozen artichoke hearts (thawed)

6 ounces cream cheese, room temperature

1 /4 cup mayonnaise

1 /2 cup grated Parmesan

salt and pepper

puff pastry, thawed

1 egg white, lightly beaten

Preheat oven to 350 °F. Lightly grease a baking sheet or cover with parchment paper.

Heat spinach in a medium sauté pan just until wilted. Add the chopped artichoke hearts and cook, stirring frequently, just until the artichoke hearts are heated through, and liquid is evaporated, about 3 minutes more. Remove the pan from the heat and immediately add the cream cheese, mayonnaise, Parmesan, salt, and pepper. Stir until evenly combined.

Roll puff pastry out on a lightly floured surface to about 15x20 inches. Using a round biscuit cutter or the top of a drinking glass, cut the pastry into even circles. (*Or you can use a pizza cutter to slice the pastry into even squares or rectangles. Any shape will work.*) Place a large spoonful of the spinach and artichoke mixture in the center of each piece of dough. With each piece of pastry, fold one side over so that the ends meet and crimp the edges to seal the filling inside. Place the hand pies on the prepared baking sheet, leaving about 3 inches of space between them. Cut a slit in the top of each hand pie and lightly brush the top with egg white. Bake until the tops of the pies are golden brown, 15-20 minutes. Serve immediately.

Chicken Pot Pie Hand Pies

Warm, luscious comfort food at the end of your wrist!

3 1/2 cups flour (wheat or white)

2 tablespoons additional flour

1 tablespoon salt, divided

1 teaspoon baking powder

10 tablespoons ice water

2/3 cup plus 2 tablespoons olive oil, divided

1 1/2 pounds ground or chopped chicken

1 cup fresh green beans, cut into 1 /4 inch pieces

3/4 cup finely chopped carrot

1 tablespoon chopped fresh thyme

1 tablespoon minced garlic

1/2 cup fresh or frozen green peas, thawed

1 1/2 cups chicken stock

1 tablespoon chopped fresh parsley, plus more for garnish

3/4 teaspoon freshly ground black pepper

1 large egg, beaten

1 teaspoon water

Combine 3 1/2 cups flour, 1 1/2 teaspoons salt, and baking powder in a food processor; pulse. Put 10 tablespoons ice-cold water and 2/3 cup oil in a glass; with processor running, slowly pour water-and-oil mixture in, mixing until dough is crumbly. Turn dough out onto a lightly floured surface. Knead 1 minute. Cover and chill 30 minutes.

Preheat oven to 400°F. Heat 1 tablespoon oil in a large nonstick skillet over medium-high heat. Cook chicken, stirring often, until no longer pink. Dump chicken and pan drippings into a bowl and set aside. Without wiping pan, heat remaining 1 tablespoon oil over medium-high; add beans, carrot, thyme, and garlic. Cook until tender. Add chicken and drippings back to pan; stir in peas. Sprinkle with remaining 2 tablespoons flour, stirring to coat. Add chicken stock and bring to a boil; cook for 3 to 4 minutes or until thickened. Fold in parsley, pepper, and remaining salt. Cool somewhat.

Divide dough into 12 equal balls. Roll each ball into a 6-inch circle on a lightly floured surface. Spoon 1/3 cup chicken mixture onto center of each circle. Brush edges of dough circles with egg wash. Fold dough over filling to form half-moons, pressing edges together to seal. Brush remaining egg mixture over tops of pies and score tops to vent. Bake on cookie sheet until golden.

Shepherd's Hand Pies

Comfort food at the end of a stressful day...or week. If you substituted ground beef for the lamb, these would be "cottage" pies. Whatever you call them, you'll call them a favorite!

Crust

4 oz. cold butter (1 stick)
4 oz. cream cheese
1 teaspoon salt
2 cups flour
1 tablespoon sugar
1/4 cup whole milk, plus 2-3 tablespoons

Cut the butter and cream cheese into 1/2-inch cubes. Combine the dry ingredients in a food processor, pulsing to combine. Add the butter and cream cheese and pulse until the mixture looks like small peas. Pour in milk, pulsing until combined. If the mixture is too dry to come together, add 2-3 more tablespoons milk, pulsing after each addition. Chill at least 30 minutes.

Filling

1 large onion, diced
2 tablespoons olive oil

1 teaspoon sugar
1/2 lb. ground lamb
2 medium carrots, diced
1 medium potato, diced (or 1/2 cup leftover
mashed potatoes)
1/2 cup frozen peas
2 cloves garlic, minced
2 sprigs fresh thyme
1 tablespoon tomato paste
1 tablespoon flour
1 cup apple juice
2 tablespoons vinegar
1 egg, beaten with 1 teaspoon water

Sauté onions with sugar and a pinch of salt until caramelized, about 15 minutes. Brown lamb, stirring to break up. Add carrots, potato, peas, garlic and thyme. Cook until vegetables are tender, about 5 minutes. Stir in tomato paste and flour and cook for 1 minute. Deglaze the pan with apple juice and vinegar, scraping brown bits off the bottom of the pan. Reduce the liquid by half, until the sauce is thick enough to coat the back of a spoon. Remove from heat and let cool slightly.

Preheat oven to 375 °F. Line 2 baking sheets with parchment paper. Working with half of the dough on a floured surface, roll the dough to 1/8 inch thick. Cut out rounds with the 3-inch biscuit cutter (two for each pie.) Spoon about a teaspoon of filling onto half of the crusts. Place the other half of the rounds atop to form a round pie. Seal the edges with a fork. Using a pastry brush, lightly coat each pie with egg wash. Bake until golden brown, about 20 minutes.

Chicago Pork Pies

Traditional Midwest hand pies, and if you've never tasted them, are you in for a treat! Unbaked pies freeze beautifully; just add a few minutes to the baking time.

2 pounds ground pork
3 garlic cloves, minced
1 teaspoons salt
1/2 teaspoon pepper
1/4 teaspoon ground cloves
1/4 teaspoon ground nutmeg
1/8 teaspoon cayenne pepper
1 tablespoon cornstarch
1-1/4 cups chicken broth
pie crust recipe
1 egg
2 teaspoons milk

Preheat oven to 425°. In a large skillet, cook pork, garlic and seasonings over medium heat until pork is no longer pink, breaking up pork. Add broth mixed with corn starch. Cook until thickened, stirring constantly. Cool slightly.

Roll pie crust dough into a rectangle. Use a round cookie to cut twenty 4-inch circles and twenty 2-

3/4-inch circles, rerolling scraps as needed. Press larger circles in a muffin pan, shaping dough up the sides of the cups. Spoon 3 tablespoons pork mixture into each muffin cup. Set small circles over filling, and seal with a fork. Whisk egg and milk together and brush each pie. Cut slits in each to vent steam. Bake 15-20 minutes or until golden brown. Serve warm.

Runza

Another regional favorite throughout the Upper Midwest, these hearty meat-and-cabbage hand pies have been making lunch munchers happy for years! The crust is a warm, soft, tasty, yeast dough. Need I go on?

Crust:

4-1/2 cups flour, divided
1/2 cup sugar
2 packets active dry yeast
1 teaspoon salt
3/4 cup milk
1/2 cup water
1/2 cup shortening or butter
2 large eggs

Filling:

1 pound lean ground beef
2 small onions, chopped
4 cups chopped cabbage
salt and pepper

Crust: Measure 1 3/4 cups flour, and the sugar, yeast and salt into a large bowl. Heat the milk, water and shortening or butter to 120° or so. Pour over flour mixture, add eggs, and beat with an

electric mixer on low until blended. Beat 3
additional minutes on high. Stir in the remaining
flour by hand. Knead until smooth and elastic,
about 6-8 minutes. Let rise in a greased bowl,
covered, until doubled.

Cook beef and onion in a large skillet until meat is
cooked through. Drain. Add the cabbage, salt and
pepper Cook, stirring, until cabbage is wilted.

Punch dough down and roll into twelve 6-inch
squares. Top each square with 1/3 cup meat
mixture. Fold corners together into triangles.
Crimp edges with a fork tightly to seal, and place
on greased baking sheets. Bake at 350 °F until
golden brown. Serve hot.

Swedish Meat Pies

Swedish meat pies actually taste best when they're not piping hot. They get better (and won't burn your mouth) after cooling for a little while. This - plus their portability -makes them great make-ahead party food! Just bake before your guests arrive.

Crust:

1 cup butter, softened

3/4 cup sour cream

2 cups flour

Pinch salt

Filling:

2 tablespoons olive oil

1 small onion, minced

2 ribs celery, chopped

1 large carrot, finely chopped

1 clove garlic, pressed

2 cups shredded potatoes, rinsed

1 pound ground beef

Freshly ground black pepper

Pinch ground nutmeg

Pinch ground allspice

2 cups shredded cheddar cheese

Crust: Beat the butter and sour cream on medium speed until smooth, using mixer. Stir in flour and salt until combined. Chill, covered, until firm, at least one hour.

Heat oil in a large skillet over medium heat. Add the onion, celery, and carrot, and sauté until the onions are translucent, about ten minutes. Add the garlic, potatoes, ground beef, salt, pepper, nutmeg and allspice. Crumble the meat, and cook until the meat is no longer pink. Remove the skillet from heat, and stir in the cheddar cheese. Cool to room temperature.

Preheat oven to 350 °F. Line two baking sheets with parchment paper. Divide the chilled dough into eight equal balls. On a well-floured surface, roll each ball into a circle about 8 inches in diameter. Place a scoop of filling on one side of a dough circle, and fold the other side over into a half-moon shape. Brush water with your finger along edge of dough, then crimp with fork to seal. Cut slit in top for steam to vent. Bake for 30 minutes, or until the crust is golden and bubbly. Allow the pies to cool somewhat before serving.

Chicken Cornish Pasties

A nice thing about hand pies is exploring regional and ethnic flavors you might overlook otherwise. Pronounced PASS tees, these hearty hand pies have a long history, going back to early tin miners. Go ahead and substitute chopped beef, pork, or lamb for the chicken next time you make them. It's your dinner!

Crust:

1 cup shortening
1 /2 cup butter at room temperature
1 1 /2 cup flour AND 1 1 /2 cup whole wheat flour
OR 3 cups flour
1 teaspoon salt
1/ 2 cup cold water

Filling:

2 tablespoons olive oil
1 1/ 2 lb ground or minced chicken
1 cup diced onion
1 tablespoon minced garlic
1 cup diced celery
1 cup diced sweet red pepper
2 cups grated carrot
2 cups grated peeled sweet potato

1/ 2 cup sour cream
1 cup chicken stock
3 tablespoons vinegar (balsamic, if you have it on hand)
1 /3 cup packed brown sugar
2 tablespoons chopped fresh rosemary
1 teaspoon dry mustard
salt and pepper
1 egg, beaten

 In a large mixing bowl, beat together shortening and butter until creamy. In a separate bowl, combine salt and flour(s). Add the flour, one cup at a time until incorporated. Pour in water all at once and mix. Knead a few times on a floured board, then cover with plastic wrap and chill.

Cook chicken in oil in a large saucepan, stirring to break up meat, until browned. Drain off excess fat. Stir in onion, garlic, celery and red pepper; cook for 5 minutes or until vegetables are tender. Add carrot, sweet potato, chicken stock, vinegar, brown sugar, rosemary, mustard, salt and pepper. Cook over medium heat, stirring frequently, until liquid has absorbed and vegetables are tender. Stir in sour cream. Cool slightly.

Preheat oven to 375 °F. Shape pastry into 12 equal balls. Roll balls into 6-inch circles on a lightly floured board. Spoon 1 /4 cup filling onto the bottom section of each circle. Brush edge of pastry with beaten egg. Fold dough over into half-moon shape and crimp the curved edge of pasty with tines of a fork. Place on prepared baking sheet, curving corners slightly. Brush with remaining egg. Bake until golden brown.

Cheese, Onion, and Potato Pasty

This cheesy pasty is a loaded with caramelized onions, a delicious step out of the ordinary. You can use pie crust in place of the puff pastry, if you prefer. Your vegetarian friends will love you!

puff pastry, thawed
1 large onion
1 tablespoon sugar
2 tablespoon butter
salt and pepper to taste
2 medium potatoes, diced
8oz. cheddar cheese
1 egg
milk

In a medium skillet, brown onion with sugar, butter, salt and pepper until onion is golden, stirring frequently. Add potato and cook until tender. Cool, then stir in cheese and egg. Cut pastry into long rectangles. Place filling along top half of pastry, blot edge with water, then fold bottom to top and crimp to seal Brush each with milk. Bake for 45 minutes.

Scottish Meat Pies

Makes six muffin-sized pies; you may as well double it, because they freeze beautifully! Don't skip the nutmeg; that's where the unique flavor comes from.

Pastry

3 1/ 3 cups flour
1 /2 teaspoon salt
1 cup water
1/2 cup butter

Filling

1 lb. ground lean beef or lamb
1 teaspoon Worcestershire sauce
half small onion, diced
1 cup dry oatmeal
1 /2 teaspoon nutmeg
1 /2 cup beef stock, bullion or broth
salt and pepper

Preheat oven to 275 °F. Bring butter and water to boil in saucepan. Pour boiling water mixture over flour and salt. Mix until combined; let rest until cool enough to handle. Knead until smooth. Roll 1 /2 inch thick on floured board. Cut circles to fit muffin pans, and ease dough into each cup, forming a ridge of dough extending above the cups. Save reserved dough. Combine all filling ingredients, and divide evenly into pastry cups. Cover with leftover pastry dough, tucking around edges to seal. Slit to vent. Brush tops with milk or beaten egg. Bake at 275 °F for 30 minutes, raise oven to 350 °F and bake another 15 minutes, until pies are golden.

Russian Beef Piroshki

The soft, eggy dough is what sets these apart from other meat pies.

1 c milk, warmed
1 tablespoon sugar
1 packet active dry yeast
3 to 3 1/4 cups flour
1 egg, room temperature
1 tablespoon salted butter, softened
hefty dash salt
1 lb lean ground beef
1 onion, chopped
salt and pepper
handful raisins
milk

In a frying pan, over medium high heat, brown the ground beef until cooked through. Add onions and continue to fry until translucent. Sprinkle in salt and pepper and raisins. Cool.

Preheat oven to 350 °F.
Divide dough into golf-ball sized balls. Roll out dough balls as thin as you can into the shape of an oval. Place a tablespoon of filling in the middle. Fold sides up into half-moon shape and securely pinch seam together at the top. Set on prepared pan, leaving a couple of inches between pies, as

they will rise in baking. Brush each piroshki with milk. Bake until golden brown, about 15 minutes.

Natchitoches Meat Pies

Natchitoches, Louisiana, southwest of Shreveport, is a place like no other, and this hand pie recipe captures the essence perfectly. These savory meat pies will be a sure favorite!

Crust:

2 1/2 cups flour
2 teaspoons salt
1/2 cup vegetable oil
1/2 cup ice water

Filling:

2 tablespoons butter
1/2 pound ground beef
2 garlic cloves, pressed
1/2 onion, diced
1/4 green bell pepper, diced
1 bay leaf
1 tablespoon tomato paste
1/4 teaspoon cayenne pepper
1/4 teaspoon ground cloves
1/4 teaspoon chopped thyme
1/8 teaspoon ground coriander
1/8 teaspoon ground allspice

Salt
Hot sauce, such as Tabasco, to taste
1 egg beaten with 2 tablespoons of milk

Using a food processor, combine the flour and salt. Add oil and process until the flour is moistened. Sprinkle ice water and pulse 5 or 6 times, just until the dough comes together. Knead on floured board until smooth. Cover and chill for 30 minutes.

In a large skillet, cook the ground beef in butter with garlic, onion, bell pepper and bay leaf over moderate heat, stirring occasionally, until beef is browned and onion is translucent. Stir in the tomato paste and seasonings and cook another three minutes. Discard bay leaf. At this point, you can either pulse filling in food processor until nearly smooth, or leave chunky. Cool.

Preheat the oven to 350 °F. Line baking sheet with parchment paper. Roll out dough on a floured board, and cut into 12 rounds using a 4 inch cutter. Place heaping spoonful of filling on center of the circles, and brush edges with egg. Fold into half-moon shape, crimping edges with a fork. Cut vent. Brush with egg. Bake for 25 minutes, until golden brown.

Gulf Coast Crawfish Hand Pie

These two-bite yummies will be a hit at your next party! With society's demand for culinary fluidity, I bet you can find crawfish in your grocer's freezer section, if you can't get them fresh. And really, how often do you get to use "culinary fluidity" in a sentence?

crust:
1 1 /2 cups flour
1/2 teaspoon salt
1 /2 teaspoon sugar
7 tablespoons cold butter, grated
up to 1 4/ cup ice water

filling:
8 oz. sliced bacon, cut into 1/4-inch pieces
2 cups shredded cheddar cheese
handful chopped chives
3 tablespoons flour
1 teaspoon salt
1/2 teaspoon pepper
1/2 cup milk
2 large eggs
8 oz. crawfish tails, cooked and chopped

Stir together crust ingredients, using just enough ice water to hold dough together. Gather into a ball and chill while filling cooks.
Cook bacon over medium heat until crisp. Drain. Combine bacon, cheese, chives, flour, salt, pepper, milk, and eggs. Gently stir in crawfish. cool.

Preheat oven to 375 °F. Roll out crust on lightly floured board. Cut twenty-four 3 1/2-inch circles, and press into 24 mini muffin cups. Prick sides and bottom of crusts with a fork to prevent bulging in the oven. Divide filling evenly among crusts.
Bake until lightly golden and puffy, about 15 minutes. Serve warm.

Open-face Turkish Hand Pies

I first tasted these delicious flat pies in Kusadasi, Turkey. I asked the waiter what kind of meat they included. He said firmly, "Meat meat.' Oh, there you go! The tender dough and unusual spices make these pies a good break from your usual menu. Don't let the long ingredient list scare you; it's worth it!

Spice Mix
(more than you need; save rest for next time)

1 tablespoon ground cloves
2 tablespoon ground black pepper
2 tablespoon ground cumin
1 /2 teaspoon salt
1 tablespoon coriander
1 teaspoon nutmeg
1 /2 tablespoon cardamom
1 /2 tablespoon cinnamon

Dough:

1 packet active dry yeast
1 /4 cup warm water
2 teaspoons sugar
2 1 /2 cups flour
dash salt
3 /4 cup yogurt (plain)

1 /4 cup olive oil

Meat Filling:

1 tablespoon olive oil
1 lb ground beef
1 onion, diced
3 cloves garlic, pressed
2 tablespoons tomato paste
2 teaspoons white or brown sugar
2 tablespoon chopped fresh mint
1 /3 cup yogurt
1 /2 teaspoon salt
toasted pine nuts, optional

Set yeast to bloom in warm water mixed with sugar. When it looks foamy, add rest of dough ingredients and knead until smooth. Dough will be soft. Oil dough, cover and let rise an hour or more. Cook ground beef in oil with onion and garlic. Once browned, add ONE tablespoon spice mix *(not all of it!!)*, tomato paste, and sugar. Cook for 2 more minutes. Stir in yogurt and salt. Cool.
Preheat oven to 400 °F. Cut dough into 12 pieces. Roll each piece, using olive oil (not flour) if it sticks, into a rough oval, about 3 to 4 inches in diameter. Set on baking sheet and spoon a couple tablespoonfuls of the meat mixture over the

dough, leaving a one-inch border. Sprinkle a few pine nuts over the meat. Bake until edges are golden, about 15 minutes. Shred mint on top before serving.

Shrimp Pastels (Canada)

These Canadian favorites are crisp, shrimp-filled, tender, and are addictive. Adding a little lemon zest to the filling makes them even more so. I warned you.

pie crust or puff pastry, thawed

2 tablespoons oil

1 tablespoon onion, chopped

2 cloves garlic, minced

12 ounces raw shrimp; shelled, deveined, roughly chopped

3 teaspoons tomato sauce

scant handful parsley, chopped

1 /4 cup grated mozzarella cheese

1/4 cup milk

salt and pepper, to taste

Preheat oven to 350 °F. Sauté garlic and onion in oil until translucent Add shrimp and tomato sauce. Cook one minute, remove from heat. Stir in milk, parsley, salt, and pepper. Cool. Mix in grated mozzarella cheese.

Cut the pastry into 2 inch squares. Spoon filling evenly in center of half of the squares, leaving a border. Top with another square, and crimp firmly with a fork Bake pastels at 350 °F until golden on parchment paper-lined baking sheet.

Spicy Jamaican Meat Pies

*The British had their plain beef turnovers;
Jamaicans livened that up with a big dash of curry
and some fiery Scotch bonnet pepper. Turmeric
makes the crust golden even before it's baked.
Make them small for appetizers or large for a
serious entree. And for goodness sake, don't touch
your eyes!*

Crust:

2 cups flour
2 teaspoons turmeric
1 /2 teaspoon salt
1 /2 cup cold butter
approx. 1 /2 cup ice water

Filling:

1 lb ground beef
5 scallions, chopped
1 /2 to 2 Scotch bonnet pepper, minced (*you might
want to wear gloves)*
1 tablespoon curry powder
1 /3 cup beef stock
1 teaspoon dry thyme
Salt, to taste

1 /2 cup dry breadcrumbs
milk or beaten egg for brushing

Mix the flour, turmeric and salt together in a large
bowl. Cut in chilled butter until it forms a crumbly
mixture. Sprinkle on barely enough cold water to
bring the ingredients together. Knead until smooth
on a lightly floured work surface. Chill, covered,
for at least 30 minutes.

Preheat oven to 400 °F. Brown the ground beef
with scallions, Scotch bonnet pepper, and curry
powder, breaking up as it cooks. Stir in stock,
thyme, and salt and simmer for 8 to 10 minutes.
Remove from heat. Stir in breadcrumbs to thicken.

Roll the chilled dough out 1/4 inch thick on a
floured board surface. Cut into five inch circles.
Plop filling evenly on rounds, leaving border on the
edge. Fold over into half-moon shape, and crimp
with a fork.
Brush with milk or egg, vent, and bake for 30 to 40
minutes, until golden.

SWEET HAND PIES

Enough with the virtuous, nutritious hand pies. Bring on dessert!! Perfect little one-bite treats, homemade toaster pastries, little tarts all your very own...they're heaven in a little crust!

Pumpkin Hand Pie Bites

All the flavors of pumpkin pie packed into a perfect autumn dessert; top with a bit of whipped cream makes them even better. Ideal for sharing with a neighbor

any pie crust recipe

8oz. cream cheese, room temperature

1 cup pumpkin puree

1/2 cup sugar

2 eggs + 1 egg for egg wash

1 teaspoon vanilla

1 teaspoon pumpkin pie spice

1 teaspoon cinnamon

Whipped cream, optional

Preheat oven to 350 °F. Grease a mini-muffin pan. Roll pie crust and cut into 3 inch rounds out. Press each circle, using fingers, into muffin pans. Brush egg wash from one egg onto edges of each pie. Beat cream cheese and sugar until smooth. Add eggs, one at a time, beating until combined. Stir in pumpkin puree, vanilla, and pumpkin pie spice. Fill each mini pie crust almost to the top. Sift cinnamon over pies. Bake for 15-20 minutes or until golden around the edges.

Pennsylvania Shoo Fly Pie Tarts

So sweet, you'll have to shoo flies away, these tender little Amish tarts will be a treat. Don't take them to a potluck, or everyone will insist you bring them every time!

Crust:
1 cup butter, softened
6 ounces cream cheese, softened
2 cups flour

Crumb Topping:

1 cup granulated sugar
1 1/2 cups all-purpose flour
1/2 cup butter, cold

Filling:

2 large eggs
1 1/2 cups firmly packed brown sugar
2 tablespoons butter, melted
1/4 teaspoon vanilla extract

Preheat oven to 400 °F. Beat softened butter and cream cheese until fluffy. Stir in flour. Rub butter into flour and sugar to make crumbs.

Shape dough into 16 balls and press into a mini muffin tin. Combine eggs, brown sugar, melted butter and vanilla and spoon into crusts. Sprinkle crumbs evenly over filling. Bake for about 20 minutes.

Blueberry Galettes

Galettes sounds terribly elegant, don't they? They're really just free-form little pies, with crusts folded up to encase the filling, leaving some exposed, just to show off. You can substitute cubed peaches for the berries; just add a little more corn starch.

2 2/3 cups flour

1 1/2 teaspoons salt

3 /4 cup oil

4 1 /2 tablespoons cold water

2 generous cups blueberries

1/4 cup sugar, plus 3 tablespoons for sprinkling

2 tablespoons cornstarch

1 lemon; zest from whole, juice from half

1 teaspoon vanilla extract

pinch of salt

1 egg mixed with 1 tablespoon water

Preheat oven to 425 °F.
Stir together flour and salt. Measure oil and water
in the same cup, and pour over flour, all at once.
Stir just until dough comes together, leaving some
white streaks. Roll pastry and cut palm-sized
circles. Re-roll scraps and cut more, placing on
baking sheets lined with parchment paper (at least
one will boil over!).

Stir together blueberries, sugar, cornstarch,
lemon zest, juice of half the lemon, vanilla, and salt
in a bowl. Evenly distribute the blueberry mixture
on the crusts, leaving a wide border. Turn up
edges, pinching to make a low rim, leaving some of
the filling exposed. Brush edges of galettes with
egg wash and sprinkle with sugar. Serve warm or
cold.

Flaky Jammy Hand Pies

SO much better than store-bought "toaster pastries," and you can make them any flavor you like. Great for after school snacks, after work out treat, or even breakfast! Sprinkles are optional, but they make the pies fun.

any pie crust or puff pastry
1/2 cup fruit jam, any variety
1 tablespoon cornstarch
1 egg, beaten
1 cup powdered sugar
1 tablespoon heavy cream or milk (or more as needed)   sprinkles, optional

Preheat oven to 400 °F. Mix jam with cornstarch. Set aside.
Roll pie crust or puff pastry on lightly floured board and cut into 3 X 5 inch strips. (You can make them larger or smaller) Spoon 1-2 tablespoons of jam mixture on one end of each strip. Brush a rectangle of egg around the jam as "glue." Fold the dry end over the end with jam. Crimp with fork to seal. Cut slit in top of each to vent steam. Bake on

parchment-lined baking sheet for 15–18 minutes, until golden. Cool.

Glaze: While jam pies cool, whisk powdered sugar and milk or cream together to make a smooth glaze. Drizzle over jammy pies, and scatter sprinkles if desired. Let glaze dry.

Apple Puff Tarts with Caramel Dipping Sauce

These are our plumber's favorite, and the grocery store's cashier's brother loves them, too. Don't ask why I know that.

puff pastry, thawed
4 apples, sliced very thin
1 cup brown sugar
1 tablespoon cinnamon or apple pie spice
1 dash salt

Caramel Dipping Sauce

1 cup brown sugar
4 tablespoons cold butter
1/2 cup half-and-half or heavy cream
pinch of salt
1 tablespoon vanilla

Make caramel sauce first; let cool. Combine brown sugar, butter, half-and-half or cream, and salt in saucepan. Cook over medium heat, stirring, 5 to 7 minutes, until thickened. It'll get thicker as it cools. Stir in vanilla, remove from heat. Set aside.

Preheat oven to 425 °F. Toss apple slices with salt and spice.

Cut puff pastry into 3-inch squares. Place on greased or parchment-lined baking sheet. Arrange apple slices on the pastry, overlapping 2-4 deep, leaving small border. Bake until pastry is puffed and golden brown. Edges will puff. Serve with caramel dipping sauce.

Strawberry-Banana Nutella Hand Pies

Warm, melty, sweet...what's not to love? Eat them fast, before the bananas brown. They're especially good bite-sized.

puff pastry, thawed, OR pie crust dough
1 banana, sliced thin
handful strawberries, sliced
1/2 cup chocolate hazelnut spread, such as nutella

Preheat oven to 375 °F. Cut pastry into squares or rectangles. Score the edges of pastry, about 1 /2 inch from sides. Prick middle of pastry several places with fork. Bake the puff pastry for about 15 minutes, until puffed and golden brown. Slightly flatten inner section of pastry with a spoon, to make a clear division of edge to middle. Smear chocolate hazelnut spread evenly in the center. Nicely arrange bananas and strawberries in a single layer. Jump in!

New Mexico Dried Fruit Hand Pies

Tart and chewy, you can taste the history in every bite! Use your favorite dried fruit, or any combination.

Crust:

2 1/2 cups flour

1 tablespoon sugar

3/4 teaspoon salt

1 cup (2 sticks) cold butter, grated (box grater is easiest)

about 6 tablespoons ice water

Filling:

2 cups mixed dried fruit, coarsely chopped

1 /2 cup orange marmalade

2 /3 cup water

Combine flour, sugar, salt and butter, and drizzle just enough water over mixture to hold it together. Pat into a disk, and chill while the filling cooks.

Stir together fruit, marmalade, and water in saucepan, and simmer until fruit is thickened and liquid is reduced. Cool.

Preheat oven to 400 °F. Roll crust to 1/3 inch, and cut into 5-inch squares. Plop a spoonful of fruit filling in the center. Fold into a triangle. Crimp edges with a fork, place on parchment-lined baking sheet, and bake until nicely browned.

Peanut Butter and Jelly Hand Pies

A childhood favorite, wrapped in a neat package. Let the kids have some, but it'll be a hit with grown-ups, too. If you use smooth PB, toss in a few chopped peanuts for crunch.

puff pastry, thawed

4 ounces cream cheese, room temperature

1/3 cup peanut butter (chunky or smooth)

3 tablespoons sugar

1 tablespoon honey (optional, but nice)

1 tablespoon milk

10 teaspoons grape jelly (or your favorite jam)

1 egg, beaten OR 2 tablespoons milk

coarse sugar, for sprinkling (optional)

Combine cream cheese, peanut butter, peanuts if using, sugar, honey, and milk. Set aside. Roll puff pastry to an 11" square. Cut out even number of circles, and place on a parchment-lined baking sheet. Spoon 1 tablespoon peanut butter filling and 1 teaspoon jelly in the middle of each round. Brush the egg or milk around the filling. Top with second round, and press to seal. Crimp edges with fork. Cut small slit in center of each hand pie. Place baking sheet in freezer for at least 30 minutes. This prevents filling from exploding (ask me how I know!).

Preheat oven to 425 °F. Brush the tops of each pie with egg or milk. Sprinkle each pie with coarse sugar. It makes them crunchy, but white sugar will do. Bake for 15 minutes at 425 °F, then lower temperature to 400°F. Bake until the pies are golden brown and bubbling (5 – 10 minutes more). Cool 10 minutes before serving. They're best enjoyed warm, but not boiling inside.

S'mores Hand Pies

Everything you love about those graham-marshmallow-chocolate treats, without the smell of a campfire in your hair. Leftovers aren't likely, but if you have any, store them, covered, in refrigerator.

1 recipe pie crust (borrow from another hand pie recipe)

8 graham cracker squares, finely crushed, about 1 /2 cup

1/4 cup sugar

3 tablespoons butter, melted

1 /2 cup marshmallow crème

2 tablespoons cream cheese, softened 2

1/2 cup chocolate chips

Preheat oven to 425° F. Line baking sheet with parchment paper. Cut pie crust into 3 inch rounds. In shallow plate, combine cracker crumbs and 1/4 cup sugar. Brush both sides of pie crust rounds

with melted butter. Coat with crumb mixture,
pressing lightly. Place crumb-coated pie crust
rounds on baking sheet. Stir marshmallow crème,
cream cheese, and chocolate chips together. Spoon
a heaping tablespoon filling in center of half of the
rounds. Set remaining crusts on top, and crimp
edged firmly with a fork. Bake 9 to 12 minutes,
until golden brown.

Addictive Lime Curd Cheesecake Tarts

With lime curd priced at about $6 a jar, here's your incentive to make your own! These cream cheese and lime curd tarts are easy, and did I mention they're ...addictive? In a pinch, substitute any sugar cookie dough for crusts, if you wish.

Lime Curd (recipe follows), cooled

Crust:

2 3/4 cups flour
1 teaspoon baking soda
1/2 teaspoon baking powder
1 cup butter, room temperature
1 1/2 cups sugar
1 egg
2 teaspoon vanilla extract
3 oz. cream cheese, softened

Preheat oven to 375 °F. Combine flour, baking soda, and baking powder. In another bowl, cream butter and sugar until smooth; beat in egg and vanilla, then gradually blend in flour mixture. Press rounded teaspoonfuls of dough into mini muffin

pans, patting across bottoms and up the sides.
Bake for about 10 minutes, just until crusts begin
to turn golden around the edges. Drop a scant
teaspoonful of cream cheese into each crust. Cool
slightly, then top with lime curd (recipe follows).
Best served chilled.

Lime Curd

*This recipe is easy and done in under 10 minutes!
Use limes, bottled key lime juice, lemon, oranges,
even grapefruit to make the perfect curd at home.
It makes a quick and easy filling for any hand pies.
It's also tasty on the end of a spoon...*

3 large eggs

3/4 cup sugar

scant pinch of salt

1/2 cup fresh lime juice (or bottled key lime
juice)

zest of 1 large or two small limes (or key limes)

4 tablespoons unsalted butter, diced

Whisk eggs, sugar, salt, juice, and zest in a
medium saucepan until smooth. Stirring
constantly with a wooden spoon, cook over medium
low heat until the mixture thickens, about 4-5
minutes. Remove from heat and add butter. Stir
until blended. Cool.

Summer Peach Hand Pies

You can substitute frozen (thawed) peaches if it's not fresh peach season when the craving hits. Stir in 1/8 tsp. almond extract for even more flavor.

any pie dough recipe OR puff pastry

1/2 cup water

2 teaspoons fresh lemon juice

1 /2 cup granulated sugar

1/8 cup cornstarch

1/4 tsp. vanilla extract

1/8 tsp. ground cinnamon

2-3 large peaches, peeled, pitted, and chopped

Stir together water, lemon juice, sugar, and cornstarch, and cook over medium heat until thickened and bubbly, about 5 minutes. Keep stirring to prevent sticking. Stir in extract(s) and cinnamon. Add peaches, stirring to coat. Let cool.

Preheat oven to 375 °F. Roll crust and cut into rectangles. Place spoonful of filling at one end, and fold dry end over. Crimp with fork, vent, brush with milk, and bake until golden brown.

Cranberry-Raisin-Orange Tarts

"Rustic" is an official cooking term, meaning "not identical." It does not mean "messy"! Made smaller, these are fabulous appetizers; zingy, not too sweet, and delicious!

Crust:

1 1/2 cups flour

1 1/2 tablespoons sugar

dash salt

6 oz. cold butter, cut into pieces

less than 3 tablespoons cold water.

Filling:

3 cups fresh cranberries

1 cup raisins

3/4 cup sugar; more to taste

1/4 cup maple syrup

zest of 1 orange

3 tablespoons fresh orange juice

dash salt

5-6 gingersnap cookies, crushed, set aside

Pulse flour, sugar, and salt in a food processor to combine; drop in butter and pulse until it resembles coarse meal. Add water, a spoon at a time, just until dough comes together. Press unto six equal balls and wrap in plastic. Chill until firm, about an hour.

Combine cranberries, raisins, sugar, maple syrup, orange zest and juice, and salt. Simmer over medium heat, stirring occasionally, until sugar has dissolved, the cranberries have popped, and mixture is thick and syrupy, about six minutes. If it's too tart, add a few more spoons of sugar, stirring to dissolve. Cool to room temperature; filling will continue to thicken.

Roll dough balls into rough 5-6 inch circles, and arrange on parchment-lined baking sheets. Sprinkle gingersnap crumbs in the center of each circle. Spoon a blob of filling on top, and fold up edges to partly cover filling. Light press dough pleats to seal. Bake until golden and bubbly.

Southern Pecan Pie Mini Tarts

Sweet and crunchy, these remind me of the Deep South's best dessert. Stir in a handful of raisins for variety next time.

3 cups chopped pecans, toasted in dry pan until fragrant

3/4 cup sugar

3/4 cup light or dark corn syrup

3 large eggs, beaten

2 tablespoons melted butter

2 teaspoons vanilla extract

dash salt

pre-baked tart shells (or frozen, baked as package directs)

Preheat oven to 350°. Set baked tart shells on pan.

Stir sugar and corn syrup until combined. Add in pecans, eggs, salt, vanilla and butter. Place tart shells on a baking sheet. Fill each tart shell about 3 /4 full. Bake at 350° for 25 to 30 minutes, until set. Cool.

Canadian Butter Tarts

Canadian Butter Tarts taste like childhood. I grew up in western New York, and my family spent summers at The Cottage on Georgian Bay, near Toronto. I always knew we were nearly there when Dad pulled into the bakery's parking lot for a box of these flakey, creamy butter tarts.

2 2/3 cups flour

1 1/2 teaspoons salt

3 /4 cup oil

4 1 /2 tablespoons cold water

2 eggs

1 cup raisins

1 cup brown sugar

1/4 cup melted butter

1 teaspoon vanilla

2 teaspoons cream

Preheat oven to 350° F.

Stir together flour and salt. Measure oil and water in the same cup, and pour over flour, all at once. Stir just until dough comes together, leaving some white streaks.

Press dough into muffin cups, rising it up the sides to form cups. Beat the eggs, then add rest of ingredients, mixing well. Fill each cup a little more than halfway (filling puffs as it bakes). Bake 20-25 minutes till golden brown.

Bridesmaid Tarts

While these luscious, lemony, ricotta-filled tarts contain no actual bridesmaids, they're a tasty bite at any occasion

puff pastry

1 cup ricotta or cottage cheese, drained briefly

3 tablespoons sugar

3 tablespoons lemon juice

zest of one lemon

2 eggs

1 tablespoon butter, melted

Preheat oven to 400° F.

Roll out puff pastry dough very thinly on a lightly floured surface, cut 12 circles, and press gently into grease muffin tins. It's okay if the circles only reach partway up the sides; do your best. Chill dough while you prepare the filling.

Beat ricotta cheese, sugar, lemon juice, and lemon zest together. Stir in eggs and butter until smooth. Prick tart crusts with a fork in several places. Spoon filling into the crusts.

Bake at 400° F for 20 minutes until puffed, golden, and no longer jiggly. Serve warm.

Lemon Coconut Tartlets

Cupped in pre-made phyllo tart shells, these couldn't be easier. Perfect for a summery dessert any time of year, especially when the weather forecast is anything but summery.

32 pre-baked phyllo cups

1 cup sugar

1 tablespoon flour

3 eggs, beaten

1 1 /2 tablespoon grated lemon peel

1/3 cup lemon juice

1/2 cup shredded sweetened coconut

Preheat oven to 375° F. Stir together sugar, flour, eggs, lemon peel and juice until combined. Press coconut gently in tart shells, using approximately 1 teaspoon in each. Spoon lemon mixture over top of coconut.

Bake 20-25 minutes, until filling is set. Cool.

Streamlined Baklava Bites

With a nice salty/sweet balance, these are much easier than making baklava! I recall my elderly aunts rolling out dough thin enough to read through, and layering it with butter and nuts. This tastes as good, and it's not a bicep workout.

1(8 ounce) package crescent roll dough

1 cup pecans, finely chopped

1/3 cup brown sugar

1 teaspoon cinnamon

1/2 teaspoon salt

1 /2 stick butter, cut into 8 slices

honey

Preheat oven to 375°F. Grease a muffin tin.

Gently press crescent dough inside each muffin cup, making sure to seal the seams, and leaving excess hanging over the edges.

Stir pecans, brown sugar, salt and cinnamon. Spoon the filling evenly into the muffin cups, gently tamping down with the back of a spoon. Place one slice of butter on top of each.

Bake for 15 minutes, until the dough is puffed and golden and the butter is melted. Serve warm with a drizzle of honey.

Drip Down Your Shirt Fresh Cherry Hand Pies

These are seriously wonderful. You can make the filling a few days in advance. Maybe you should double it; it's mighty good on the end of a spoon, too!

1 box (2 sheets) frozen puff pastry, thawed

1 large egg beaten with 2 teaspoons milk

coarse sugar for garnish

Filling

1 and 1/2 tablespoons cornstarch

2 tablespoons water

12 ounce bag frozen cherries OR 2 1/4 cups fresh cherries, pitted

1/2 cup granulated sugar

1 teaspoon fresh lemon juice

1/8 teaspoon salt

1 teaspoon vanilla extract

In a medium saucepan, combine the cherries, sugar, lemon juice, and salt. Stir occasionally, cooking over medium heat until the cherries begin to release their juice, about 4-6 minutes. Combine cornstarch and water, stir in, and bring to a boil, stirring constantly. Boil one minute, then remove from heat. Stir in vanilla. Cool.

On a lightly floured surface, roll out pastry sheets and cut 6 rectangles from each. Lay half on parchment-lined baking sheet. Spoon 2-3 tablespoons of cooled filling in middle of rectangles. Place the top rectangles over the filling, vent, and crimp edges firmly with a fork.

Brush the tops of the pastry pies with egg wash, then sprinkle with coarse sugar. Chill the pies in the refrigerator for at least half an hour.

Preheat oven to 375°F.

Bake the pastry pies for 30-35 minutes, until golden brown. Cool before moving anywhere!

I hope you enjoy these delicious hand pies. Make a new tradition! Don't forget to leave a review.

Other Fun Cookbooks By Deb Graham

Hungry Kids Campfire Cookbook

Kid Food On A Stick

Quick and Clever Kids' Crafts

Awesome Science Experiments for Kids   (snack recipes included)

Savory Mug Cooking

Other Books by Deb Graham

Peril In Paradise   a cruise novel

Murder on Deck   a cruise novel

121

Tips From The Cruise Addict's Wife

More Tips From The Cruise Addict's Wife

Mediterranean Cruise With The Cruise Addict's Wife

Alaskan Cruise by the Cruise Addict's Wife

How To Write Your Story

How To Complain...and get what you deserve

Uncommon Household Tips

a few cutesy names: the plumber's pie, grocery

clerk's favorite brother's favorite pie, go kiss

somebody pie, realtor's special, share with a

neighbor, new neighbor, church potluck baby

shower teach-the-boy-to-measure, Out The Door,

big fat Greek, etc superlatives: marvelous, melt in

your mouth, on the run, busy morning. Occasions:

holiday, showered, summer afternoons, tea parties,

picnics

Made in the USA
Middletown, DE
02 October 2024

61951048R00068